SCIENCE CORNER

Weather and Seasons

Alice Harman

WAYLAND

Explore the world with **Popcorn** - your complete first non-fiction library.

Look out for more titles in the Popcorn range. All books have the same format of simple text and striking images. Text is carefully matched to the pictures to help readers to identify and understand key vocabulary.
www.waylandbooks.co.uk/popcorn

First published in 2013 by Wayland
Copyright © Wayland 2013

Wayland
Hachette Children's Books
338 Euston Road
London NW1 3BH

Wayland Australia
Level 17/207 Kent Street
Sydney NSW 2000

Produced for Wayland by
White-Thomson Publishing Ltd
www.wtpub.co.uk
+44 (0)843 208 7460

Editor: Alice Harman
Designer: Clare Nicholas
Picture researcher: Alice Harman
Series consultant: Kate Ruttle
Design concept: Paul Cherrill

British Library Cataloguing in Publication Data
Harman, Alice.
   Weather and seasons. -- (Science corner)(Popcorn)
   1. Seasons--Juvenile literature. 2. Weather--Juvenile
   literature.
   I. Title II. Series
   508.2-dc23

   ISBN: 978 0 7502 7765 5

Wayland is a division of Hachette Children's Books,
an Hachette UK company.
www.hachette.co.uk

Printed and bound in China

Picture/illustration credits:
Alamy: Fiona Deaton 11; Peter Bull 23; Stefan Chabluk 7, 8; Dreamstime: Logray 6, Benis Arapovic 10, Marian Mydlo 14, Sarah Nicholl 16/22mr, Lucian Coman 17; Shutterstock: Peter Wey cover, Anettphoto 1/13/22ml, Nejron Photo 2/18, JaySi 4, FotoYakov 5, poganyen 9/22tl, krechet 12, Terry Yarrow 14–15/22tr, Eric Gevaert 15, Nejron Photo 18/22bl, Cindy Haggerty 19, oliveromg 20/22br; Super Stock: Juniors 21.

Every effort has been made to clear copyright. Should there be any inadvertent omission, please apply to the publisher for rectification.

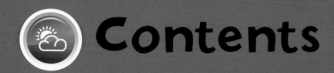# Contents

What are weather and seasons?

Weather is what we call the day-to-day changes in clouds, sunshine, wind, rain, temperature and many other natural things.

What we do depends on the weather. You may not want to go for a bike ride in the wind and rain!

There are four seasons. These are spring, summer, autumn and winter. Each season has its own type of weather.

Trees change through the year as the weather changes.

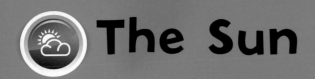 # The Sun

The Sun is a star. It is the closest star to Earth. It gives us light and heat. Sunny days are bright and warm.

You must never look straight at the Sun, as it can badly hurt your eyes.

6

The Earth circles the Sun.
It takes one year to go once
round the Sun. The Earth is
tilted as it goes round.

When one side of the world is tilted
towards the Sun, it is summer there.

At **Christmas**
time, it is
winter in the
UK and summer
in Australia.

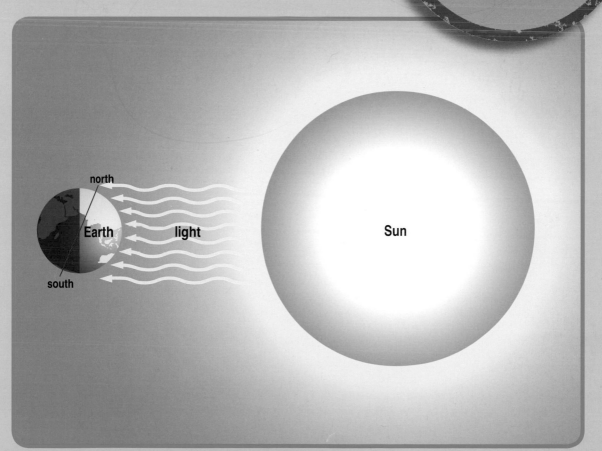

north

Earth   light   Sun

south

Clouds and rain

Clouds are made of water vapour
that comes from water in rivers and
oceans. The Sun heats the water
and it turns into water vapour.

Water vapour is invisible as it rises through the air.

clouds

rain

river

soil

lake

ocean

The air high up in the sky is cold. The water vapour in the clouds turns back into water. This water falls as rain.

We need rain for plants to grow well.

Snow and ice

In very cold weather, the rain from the clouds freezes and falls as snow or hail. Hail is hard pieces of frozen water.

When lots of snow has fallen in the mountains, people can go skiing.

When it is very cold, the water in some rivers and lakes turns to ice. The surface freezes first, and the water below mostly stays liquid.

Ducks eat water plants and insects, so it can be difficult for them to find food if the water freezes over.

11

 Wind and storms

The wind is air that is moving.
It is invisible but it can move
things that you can see. It blows
clouds from one place to another.

Very strong wind can rip trees out of the ground!

In a storm, the wind is strong and moves very fast. Lots of rain falls from big, dark clouds. There are flashes of electricity that are called lightning.

After you see lightning, you hear thunder. Thunder is the sound caused by lightning.

The temperature of a lightning bolt is hotter than the surface of the Sun!

Spring

In spring, we have more sunlight than in winter because our side of the Earth is tilted closer to the Sun. It gets warmer, and there is quite a lot of rain.

Trees start to get new leaves in spring. They sometimes also have flowers, which are called blossoms.

Plants grow well because of the sunshine and rain. Baby animals are born, because it is easier for their parents to find food in the spring than in the cold winter.

Bluebells cover forest floors in spring, and the fields are full of baby lambs.

 # Summer

Summer is the hottest time of year. The Sun is very bright and hot in the middle of the day. It gets light early in the morning, and stays light until late at night.

Many people go to the beach when it is warm and sunny.

Remember to put on sun lotion if you are out in the sunshine!

The sunlight helps plants grow flowers and fruit. There is very little rain in summer, so plants can become too dry without extra water.

Plants need water to stay alive and grow well.

Autumn

In autumn, leaves turn yellow, orange, red and brown as they die and then fall off the trees. There is often rain and strong wind, and it starts to get cold.

It's fun to play in the leaves, but keep warm with a hat and scarf!

Fruits, nuts and seeds become ripe. Animals eat a lot now, because in winter it is harder for them to find food.

Squirrels bury nuts underground in autumn so they can dig them up to eat during winter.

Winter

Winter is the coldest time of the year. There can be snow, ice and hail. Many trees lose all their leaves.

Trees that keep their leaves all year round are called evergreens.

When it is very cold, snow does not melt on the ground. That means snowballs and snowmen!

Some animals hibernate in winter, which means they sleep deeply until spring. Some plants rest underground until spring, and others die off completely.

Animals get very fat before they hibernate. This means they don't need to eat until spring.

Picture match

There are lots of different words to remember when talking about weather and seasons. Try to match each picture below to the word that best describes it.

a.

b.

c.

d.

e.

f.

1. lightning
2. snow
3. autumn
4. summer
5. rain
6. spring

22

Make a wind sock

You can use a wind sock to see which way the wind is blowing, and how fast the wind is moving.

1. Use the crayons or colouring pencils to decorate your sheet of coloured paper on one side. Roll the paper into a tube so that the edges touch, and stick it together with tape.

2. Cut the tissue paper into long strips, and stick them to one end of the paper tube.

3. Ask an adult to help you punch two holes near the other end of the paper tube. The holes should be directly across from each other.

4. Thread the string through the punched holes, to make a large loop. Cut the string to size, and tie a knot in both ends. Hang your wind sock on a tree outside, and watch it move in the wind!

23

Glossary

forest large area of trees

invisible something that we can't see

liquid something that isn't a gas or a solid, and can flow or be poured

melt change from solid to liquid, such as when ice changes to water

natural made by the Earth, not by humans

ripe fully grown, and ready to be eaten

skiing sport in which people slide on their feet down a snowy mountain

surface top layer of something

temperature measurement of how hot or cold it is

tilted not straight, leaning to one side

water vapour when water gets very hot, it turns from a liquid into a gas called water vapour

Index

EXPLORE THE WORLD WITH THE POPCORN NON-FICTION LIBRARY!

- Develops children's knowledge and understanding of the world by covering a wide range of topics in a fun, colourful and engaging way
- Simple sentence structure builds readers' confidence
- Text checked by an experienced literacy consultant and primary deputy-head teacher
- Closely matched pictures and text enable children to decode words
- Includes a cross-curricular activity in the back of each book

WATCH OUT! — ear Water — Honor Head

HISTORY CORNER — The Great Fire of London — Jenny Powell

SCIENCE CORNER — Sound and Hearing — Angela Royston

FAMILIES — My Mum — Katie Dicker

GOOD FOOD — Vegetables — Julia Adams

PEOPLE WHO HELP US — Police — Honor Head

PEOPLE WHO HELP US — irefighters — Honor Head

GEOGRAPHY CORNER — Rainforests — Ruth Thomson

A YEAR OF FESTIVALS — Muslim Festivals — Honor Head

HISTORY CORNER — The Gunpowder Plot — Jenny Powell

IN SPACE — Planets — Chris Oxlade

SEASONS — Winter — Kay Barnham

FREE DOWNLOADS!

- Written by an experienced teacher
- Learning objectives clearly marked
- Provides information on where the books fit into the curriculum
- Photocopiable so pupils can take them home

www.waylandbooks.co.uk/downloads